A Catholic Bishop Teaches…

Draw Near to Me, O Lord:
Heartfelt Prayers for Everyday Life

His Eminence
Francis Cardinal Arinze

Published by
Basilica Press
111 Fergus Court, Ste. 102
Irving, TX 75062

This book contains numerous footnotes. Their purpose is to assist readers with their prayers and formation, especially with respect to Scripture. St. Jerome said, and the Church has since unfailingly taught, "Ignorance of Scripture is ignorance of Christ." Since the purpose of prayer is to grow in our relationship with Christ, and since this happen more fully with an intimate knowledge of Scripture, it is hoped the reader will put the footnotes to good use.

Editors: Carolyn Klika and Brian O'Neel
Cover design: Giuliana Gerber (ACI Prensa-Peru)

Printed in the United States of America
ISBN 9781930314115

Basilica Press is part of the
Joseph and Marie Daou Foundation

TABLE OF CONTENTS

FOR VIRTUES   52

SOLIDARITY WITH OTHERS   59

CHURCH AND SOCIETY   65

INTRODUCTION

I. Origin of this booklet...

The origin of this booklet is as follows:
Representatives of the Sodality of Christian Life came to me and asked that I write down for them some tips, types, and patterns on personal prayer. They said that people very often want to pray but can find themselves rather dry, without words. They believed some sample prayers could help them in the ordinary situations of daily life.

I accepted their invitation. It is true that personal prayer is not, above all, talking to God, much less trying to lecture Him. It is primarily being in His presence, listening to Him, loving Him, adoring and thanking Him, requesting pardon, and asking for our temporal and spiritual needs. However, under the guidance of the Holy Spirit, even our sighs and groanings can manifest themselves in words.[1] The Paraclete helps us put our inner state of mind into words that in turn can help to focus and promote our attention and prayer.

The members of the Sodality of Christian Life, who made the request, later spelled out for me nearly 60

---

1 Cf. Rom 8:26

situations in daily life around which the sample prayers in this booklet are woven. I tried to imagine myself in those situations that they listed and to suggest prayers as near to the ordinary man or woman of today as I could imagine.

These prayers are not models, they are tips. They are suggestions to help jump-start personal prayer in the ordinary man or woman of today.

2. Pray Always

Our beloved Lord and Savior Jesus Christ taught us always to pray and to never become discouraged.[2] St. Paul tells the Thessalonians, "Always be joyful; pray constantly; and for all things give thanks; this is the will of God for you in Christ Jesus."[3]

Our Lord could not have meant formal prayers to be said always. Physically, it is not possible for us humans. Psychologically, it is not even advisable to try. We have our work to do. We need times of rest, times to eat, to play, and to chat with our family and friends. Moreover, our faculties are limited, and we are not able to concentrate expressly on many things at a time.

2 Cf. Luke 18:1
3 1 Thes 5:16-18

However, our Lord's directive stands. Jesus must have meant that we are to have a spirit of prayer, that we are not to surrender or to give up when we think our prayer is not answered, and that we are to persevere in approaching God in prayer. Indeed our whole life should be like a flowering of our love for God. The spirit of prayer should pervade our whole lives.

3. Three Kinds of Prayer

To make the purpose of this booklet clear and precise, let us distinguish three kinds of prayer.

First, there is liturgical prayer. This is the public worship of the Church. It is offered by the whole Church, and the chief person praying is Jesus Christ Himself. He associates His Mystical Body (i.e., His Spouse, the Church),[4] with Him in every liturgical prayer.[5] This prayer is formulated by the Church. The rite according to which it is to be offered is regulated by the Church.[6] Liturgical prayer is obviously of the highest order.[7]

4 Cf. 2 Cor 11:2

5 Cf. *Mediator Dei (MD)*, no. 20, encyclical, Pius XII, November 20, 1947

6 Cf. *MD*, nos. 9, 58; Cf. *Sacrosanctum Concilium (SC)*, no. 22.1, Second Vatican Council, December 4, 1963; Cf. *Mysterium Fidei (MF)*, no 24, encyclical, Paul VI, September 3, 1965

7 *MD* no. 37; *Lumen Gentium*, no. 11, Second Vatican Council, November 21, 1964; *MF*, no 38; St. Thomas Aquinas, *Summa Theologica*, IIIa, p. 73, a.3, c

Then there is community prayer. Such prayer is said by a family, a religious congregation, a Catholic movement or association, a pilgrimage center or other group in its name. Examples are morning and night prayers said by a family, prayer particular to a group such as those just named, the rosary, and the Way of the Cross.

Finally, there is personal prayer. This is the prayer that wells up from the heart of an individual. It can be in words, or it may be in the form of "inexpressible groanings,"[8] as the Holy Spirit may lead each soul. Every person's personal prayer by definition will be like that person. Your personal prayer cannot and need not be my personal prayer.

In this booklet, we are speaking only of personal prayer and not of liturgical or communal prayer.

4. Importance of Personal Prayer

Liturgical and communal prayers do not replace personal prayer. It is important that each person who takes part in the liturgy or in communal prayer pray with heart and mind. This requires an effort to make the prayer one's own, to internalize the prayer, to develop interior states

---

8 Rom 8:26

of soul that are in line with the words of the liturgical or communal prayer. The liturgical books themselves advise that there be moments of silence before and after the liturgical acts and even within them in order to help the participants to engage in silent meditation and personal prayer (such as before the Collect, after the readings, after the homily, and after Holy Communion).[9]

If personal prayer and meditation are set aside, there is the danger that liturgical and communal prayers can degenerate into ritualism, that is, a merely external carrying out of rites.[10] The prophet Isaiah already condemned this.[11] And Our Lord insisted on the same point: "This people honors Me with their lips, but their hearts are far from Me; in vain do they worship Me, teaching as doctrines human precepts."[12]

5. Usefulness of Sample Personal Prayers

The reader may now reasonably ask, "If my personal prayer is indeed to be like me, what is the use of my reading a sample personal prayer prepared by

---

9 Cf. *General Instruction on Roman Missal* 56, 66, 88, 127, 136, 105; Cf. *SC*, no. 20; Cf. *Redemptionis Sacramentum*, no. 39, instruction, Congregation for Divine Worship

10 St. Teresa of Avila and the great spiritual directors recommend spending 5-30 minutes daily in meditative prayer.

11 Cf. Is 29:13

12 Cf. Matt 15:8-9

someone else? Am I to make personal to me the prayer of St. Thomas Aquinas or St. Bonaventure or St. Francis of Assisi? How can I aspire to pray the personal prayer of such spiritual heavyweights as St. Teresa of Avila or St. John of the Cross or of St. Thérèse of Lisieux or even of saints nearer to our times such as Bl. Mother Teresa of Kolkata (formerly Calcutta)? Is it not better and safer for me to ask the Holy Spirit to teach me how to pray?"

My answer is that the reader has made an important point. Nevertheless, the reader has also to be reminded that the Holy Spirit can use human instruments to teach us how to pray. The Apostles themselves asked the Lord Jesus to teach them how to pray.[13] The great founders of monasteries and religious families taught those who gathered around them to share their spiritual charism on how to pray. The art and habit of prayer can be learned. Other people can give us tips, the benefit of their experiences, a share of what they have learned from others, possible answers to people's doubts and perplexities, and suggestions on how to leave ourselves open to divine action.

---

13 Cf. Luke 11:1

6. Holy Scripture Encourages Us

There are in Sacred Scripture many examples of personal prayer that encourage us. Abraham prayed for a son.[14] He prayed for God's mercy on Sodom and Gomorrah (although these two cities of sin were destroyed by fire because not even 10 just men could be found in them).[15] Moses interceded for the whole people.[16] Hannah, the wife of Elkanah, prayed for a child.[17] David poured out his heart in a magnificent prayer of thanksgiving when God promised that He would build for David a kingdom that would never lack an heir.[18] Solomon came out with a beautiful prayer at the dedication of the Temple.[19] When he was called by God, the prophet Jeremiah prayed, "Sovereign Lord, I don't know how to speak, I am too young." But God reassured him and sent him on a difficult prophetic mission. 19 Esther poured forth a beautiful prayer to God for her people's safety. 20 Most of the 150 Psalms are songs of praise, but some are prayers of lamentation, supplication, and even desolation. They teach us. They encourage us.

---

14 Cf. Gen 15:2-3
15 Cf. Gen 18:16-33
16 Cf. Ex 32:11-15
17 Cf. 1 Sam 1:1-18
18 Cf. 2 Sam 7:18-29
19 Cf. 1 Kings 8:22-61

The New Testament presents us with such model prayers and elevations of the heart as those of Elizabeth,[20] Zechariah,[21] Simeon,[22] the Centurion,[23] the Blind Man,[24] Zacchaeus,[25] and St. Dismas the Good Thief.[26] The *Magnificat* of the Blessed Virgin Mary has an elevation and dignity all its own.[27] Our Lord Himself taught the model of all prayer, the Lord's Prayer, at the request of the Apostles.[28] The night before He died on the Cross, Jesus offered to His Eternal Father that special prayer which occupies the entire chapter 17 of St. John's Gospel.

7. Prayer, a Gift, a Grace from the Holy Spirit

It is important that we bear in mind that although some contribution is expected from us for our prayer, nevertheless prayer is above all a gift, a grace from the Holy Spirit. The Spirit of God moves our innermost hearts and teaches us how to pray. We receive Him at Baptism. He guides us in the words, the gestures or simply

---

20 Cf. Luke 1:42-45
21 Cf. Luke 1:67-79
22 Cf. Luke 2:29-32
23 Cf. Matt 8:8-9; Luke 7:6-8
24 Cf. Luke 18:41
25 Cf. Luke 19:1-10
26 Cf. Luke 23:42
27 Cf. Luke 1:46-55
28 Cf. Matt 6:9-13

the thoughts, the elevations of the heart that contribute to our encounter with God in prayer. Our prayer can therefore be in words or without words.

St. Paul tells the Romans that it is the Holy Spirit that enables us to cry out, "Abba, Father."[29] "The Spirit Himself joins with our spirit to bear witness that we are children of God."[30] "When we do not know how to pray properly, then the Spirit personally makes our petitions for us in groans that cannot be put into words."[31]

The *Catechism of the Catholic Church* is therefore able to say, "Christian prayer is a covenant relationship between God and man in Christ. It is the action of God and of man, springing forth from both the Holy Spirit and ourselves, wholly directed to the Father, in union with the human will of the Son of God made man."[32]

The more we subject ourselves to the action of the Holy Spirit in us, the more authentic will be our prayer, and our lives will become more and more a prayer, with or without words.

Here, then, you will find over 60 suggestions to jump-start, encourage, or give us ideas on personal prayer.

---

29 Gal 4:6
30 Rom 8:15-16
31 Rom 8:26
32 *Catechism of the Catholic Church*, no. 2564

For easy reference, I have classified them to cover various situations. It is my hope that you will join me in fervent and frequent prayer for your own needs and the needs of the world. Be assured of my continued prayers.

May God's richest blessings be with you as you seek Him more intimately in prayer.

+ Francis Cardinal Arinze
Vatican City
December 22, 2005

❧ PRAYERS FOR THE DAY ❧

1. Thank God for a New Day

Lord God, a new day dawns. It is a gift of Your creating hand. You are giving me this gift of another 24 hours to be at Your service and to be in solidarity with my neighbor.

I thank You for this providential design of Yours. May every thought, word, or deed of mine in this day be pleasing to You, be according to Your will, and be my own "yes" to the unfolding of Your plan for me, for my dear ones, for the people for whom or with whom I work and indeed for all humanity.

Help me, Lord, to overcome my basic defects and weaknesses. May I show the hand of togetherness to every brother or sister with whom I am in contact today. At the end of this day, may I be able to look back with gratitude and joy and without regret. This I beg You, through Christ our Lord. Amen.

2. Thank God at Midday

God our Creator, at the middle of the day I turn to You. Engaged at Your service and the service of my neighbor since the morning, I now find myself needing a break. Some of the tasks to which I have laid my hands these past hours may have been well done. To You be thanks and praise. In others, I may have failed or been less than fully efficient. For these I beg Your forgiveness, Your healing, and Your re-creating hand. May every thought, word, and deed of mine be according to Your will, Your law, Your precepts, and Your ways.

Aware that the other half of this day is my opportunity to serve You better, I pray for Your strengthening hand, Your assisting grace, and Your accompanying peace. After this midday pause, I want to continue to give my best to You and to my neighbor, who is my path to You.

To You, Lord, through the intercession of the Blessed Virgin Mary and of St. Joseph, I offer the rest of this day as a sign of my obedience and love. Bless my little efforts, and keep me always in Your grace, through the merits of Jesus Christ our Lord and Savior. Amen.

3. Thank God at the End of the Day

Lord, the day You gave me has ended. The darkness of night descends as part of Your providential design.

I thank You for the opportunities You have given me today to live in Your service and that of my neighbor. What I may have done well, I beg You to purify, elevate, and accept through Christ, with Christ, and in Christ. What I have not done well, I beg You to correct so that everything may finally turn out to Your greater glory, the good of my neighbour, and my own spiritual growth.

Night rest and sleep are Your gift. May I have the blessing of being refreshed by rest and sleep so that I may be better able to serve You. I am joyfully confident of Your love and protection.

I pray also for all the people who find rest and sleep difficult, for those who are obliged to work long hours with little time for rest, and for those who have turned the night into a time of restless activities that are not always according to Your will. Lord, curb the devil and all forces of evil that operate more at night so that we may be better disposed to serve You when a new day dawns. To You be honor and glory, through Christ our Lord. Amen.

4. Examination of Conscience at Night

Lord my God, as I prepare to go to rest, I look back at how I have served You this day. I pray You to help me examine my conscience and see myself a little nearer to how You see me.

Has love of You and Your service been the directing motivation of all my actions this day? Have I given You adoration and praise by every thought, word, and deed? Has any action of mine been against Your will, even in small things?

How have I shown my neighbor genuine Christian love today? Have I failed to show love to my neighbor? Have I sinned in any way against anyone?

Have I made effort to combat my predominant fault? Have my prayer life and my work been in union? Has the Holy Eucharist been the center of my life?

I repent, Lord, for all my failings. I beg forgiveness by the intercession of the Blessed Virgin Mary and of my Guardian Angel. Give me a good night's rest, Lord, and the grace to serve You better tomorrow, through Christ our Lord. Amen.

❧ PRAYERS FOR MARRIAGE AND FAMILY ❧

5. Prayer for a Suitable Marriage Partner

Lord God, marriage and family are of Your divine institution. You created Adam and gave him Eve to be his wife, helper, and partner.[33]

Lord God, Creator, as I plan for marriage and the family, I kneel before You to beg for Your choice for me of the marriage partner whom Your loving Providence destines for me. May I find a person who can form a happy couple with me, procreate children for Your honor and glory, and grow with me in holiness and human maturity.

May the person share with me a firm commitment to our Catholic faith and a desire to live it and share it. May the Blessed Virgin Mary, Queen of the Family, intercede for me in the quest of such a partner and obtain for me a happy and peaceful married life to Your honor and glory. Amen.

---

33 Cf. Gen 1:27-28, 2:18, 21-25

6. Prayer for Newlywed Spouses

Lord God, we are thankful to You for uniting us recently in the Sacrament of Matrimony and calling us to reflect the union and love which exist between Christ and the Church.[34]

We thank You Lord for Your goodness. We want to love each other and sacrifice ourselves for each other and thus grow in Your love daily. May our marriage be our road to holiness, joy, peace, and human growth.[35]

You have provided that children would enter this world through the family. Keep us open to new life. Help us realize the honor and dignity You give us by calling on us to share in Your design to give new life through procreation. May we both be respectful of Your will and rejoice in our children.

Merciful God, give us friends to help us all our days as married people. May we have reasonable work and economic means to discharge our duties. Protect us from evil of every kind. Make us generous in giving to the needs of the Church and society. This we ask of You, through Christ our Lord. Amen.

---

34 Cf. Eph 5:21-33

35 Cf. *Arcanum*, nos. 9, 26, encyclical, Leo XIII, February 10, 1880; Cf. *Casti Connubii,* no. 23, encyclical, Pius XI, December 31, 1930; Cf. *Gaudium et Spes*, no. 49, Second Vatican Council, December 7, 1965; Cf. *Familiaris Consortio*, nos. 12-13, apostolic exhortation, John Paul II, November 22, 1981

7. Prayer When Difficulties Arise in Marriage

Lord our God, our married life has come up against some difficulties. Some of them may arise because of problems of adjustment in the characters of both of us in our effort to build up a harmonious household. Some challenges may be due to economic difficulties. We do not exclude our personal weaknesses, defects, or sins. It may also be that some relative or another person is more part of the problem than a source of help. We are aware that we may not even be recognizing the true source of our difficulties.

Whatever the source of difficulties or challenges, we kneel at Your feet, O Lord, to beg for light, courage, generosity of heart, the grace of forgiveness or reconciliation, and a fresh beginning each day. May we never surrender in front of these challenges. May we be spared the affliction of coldness towards each other. Rather, may we reach greater heights of mutual love through the mutual overcoming of these challenges and problems. May our union with You seal the union between us.

Mary ever Virgin and St. Joseph, pray for us, and obtain for us the grace of daily growth in marital love. Amen.

8. Prayer for a Person Tempted to Abortion

Lord God, I pray for a dear person who is now tempted to have an abortion. You know the agony experienced by this woman and others who are to some extent involved. They are tempted to regard this unborn child as unwanted. Some people have advised them to seek what they call a termination of the pregnancy.

Their agony is real, and yet, Lord, no human being should be termed "unwanted." No matter the circumstances of the conception of this child, this new human being is innocent and has the right to live.

May human solidarity come to the aid of the expectant mother and all others involved. If they cannot keep and maintain the child in the family, may at least some brother or sister pilgrim in this life come forward to offer to adopt this child. May this child live.

Show me, Lord, what I can personally do in order to show this solidarity to my friends in need. To You, God of life, be honor and glory for ever and ever. Amen.

9. Prayer When One is Far from the Family

I am, Lord, far away from my family for reasons of work, travel, study, meeting, trade, or other legitimate purpose. I think of the members of my family. I would very much like to be together with them very soon.

Lord our God, You have made the family the way of human growth, joy, peace, and holiness for the spouses, the children, and any others who live or work with them. Protect us all even as we are for the moment separated. Save every one of us from any action that may damage the unity, harmony, beauty, and sanctity of the family.

Reunite us again very soon, Lord, so that we embrace one another again, eat and play together, every evening pray our family rosary together, and commend ourselves to You for Your blessing.

May the Holy Family of Nazareth, of Jesus, Mary, and Joseph be our model. To You be the honor and glory for ever and ever. Amen.

10. Prayer to Request a Child

God our Father, all parenthood comes from You. You give father and mother the joy and honor to cooperate with Your creating hand in the origins of a new human being.

Kneeling before You, my spouse and I are begging You for the gift and joy of a child. May our home be graced by the comforting cry of a newborn child. May this sign that You have not despaired of humanity, no matter its deficiencies, come to brighten our home.

For this child we are praying that he or she be gifted with good health, growing intelligence, and an excellent religious disposition. We are thinking of a child who will be a jewel and smiling joy for the parents, a precious and appreciated citizen of society, a holy member of the Church, and a credit to any circles that find him or her a co-worker or contributor.

Lord God, in Your mercy may these graces be ours, through Christ our Lord. Amen.

11. Thank God for Our Children

God our Father, from You all parenthood has its origin and point of reference. As a Trinity of Love and Life, You Father love Your Son, the Son loves You, and the Holy Spirit is the personification of Your mutual love.

Children are Your gift. You have kindly allowed us to be parents. We thank You, Lord, for any children that You give us. In them, we see Your blessing bestowed on us. In them, You allow us to live on. In their arrival, we see Your declaration that You have not abandoned humanity, that You want humanity to continue.

Thank You Lord, for these children whom You have given us. May each of them grow in wisdom and grace. May they grow up to make excellent contributions to Church and society.

We pray, Lord, for their vocation and mission in the Church and in the world. If Your providence calls some of them to the priesthood or the consecrated life, it will be a great honor for this family. May this family prepare them in the best possible way for their future. Bless them. Bless this family. Bless all children. Bless all families, in Christ Jesus our Lord. Amen.

12. Prayer for the Physical, Moral, and Spiritual Health of Children

Lord God, as our children grow up, we are concerned about their good health in every sense of the word: physical, intellectual, moral, and spiritual. We want them to grow up as good children in the family, a credit to the Church, and enviable contributors to the progress of society.

We are aware that many influences play on the children. It is not only our family, but also the school, the mass media, and society as a whole that influence them. We shall continue to do what we can to contribute to the state of our school, media, and society so that these arenas will not undermine the good formation that our family is striving to provide.

Our efforts are not enough to secure the desired result. We pray You, Lord, to raise enough people in our society to join hands for the provision of the best possible conditions for the growth of our children.

Lord Jesus, You grew up as a Child in the Holy Family of Nazareth. Please protect our children and bless them. Guide our society now and ever after. Amen.

13. Prayer for a Sick Child

Lord Jesus, our child is sick! We are making what efforts we can to see the doctor and to show our child our love and concern. We are in agony, Lord.

You love children. During Your public ministry, You rebuked those who were trying to keep the children away from You. You called the children to Yourself, imposed Your hands on them, and blessed them.[36]

Come now, Lord Jesus, to impose Your hands on our sick child. Enable the doctor to see exactly what is wrong and to apply the required and adequate remedy. May our dear child soon recover fully to his own joy and that of his parents, brothers and sisters, and playmates. Lord, You know that as parents we prefer to suffer rather than see our child suffer.

Mary Immaculate, Mother in the Holy Family of Nazareth, intercede for our sick child with Your Divine Son.

May this child soon get well again to praise the Lord. Amen.

---

36 Cf. Mark 10:14-16

14. Prayer for a Wayward Child

Lord God, one of my children is not doing well in religious matters. He rarely attends Sunday Mass. He does not go to Confession. He finds it hard to join the rest of the family in our daily family prayers. Moreover, I fear that he may be engaging in activities and associating with people who are leading him farther from You, especially since there are groups that have a bad name in society and have damaged many children. My child finds it harder and harder to listen to advice from his parents.

Help me, Lord. You accepted the tears of St. Monica for her erring son Augustine. After many years, Your overpowering grace brought Augustine to conversion. Mercifully receive my pains and anguish, my anxieties and sleepless nights for the conversion of my child. May I have the joy of seeing him take religion more seriously and offer You loving worship.

St. Monica, pray for us. Amen.

15. Prayer When Bringing Children to School

Lord God, as we bring our children to school this day, we pray for Your blessing on them in this educational institution. May the school help them to develop their faculties and abilities in the best direction. Along with intellectual and physical growth, may they make progress in moral and religious development.

Sometimes there are forces in school that undermine rather than help the efforts of the family to promote the moral and religious growth of the children. May such forces not rear their heads in this school. Gift the teachers with the best performance in these and other directions.

When we return in the afternoon to collect our children, may we find them positively making the desired progress. May this blessing descend on our children and on all children in the schools in this country, and indeed in the whole world.

St. John Bosco, great educator of children, pray for our children and for all school children everywhere. Amen.

16. Thank God for My Parents

Lord God, Creator, in Your beautiful Providence You have arranged that every child will have a father and a mother. The parents are the greatest earthly gift that You provide for children.

I thank You for the parents You have given me. Under Your creating hand, they brought me into this world. They have made many sacrifices for my birth, nourishment, nursing care, and the many needs of a growing child. They arranged my school education. They have taught me above all to love You and to serve You, and they have helped me to enter into the wider society.

Bless my parents, Lord. Give them the joy of seeing their children grow in wisdom and grace before God and people. May we their children be their support especially in their old age.

Lord Jesus Christ, You loved and honored Your Virgin Mother and Joseph, Your foster father. Teach me to be a consolation to my parents and always to love, honor, and obey them.

Lord God, I pray for all parents who have difficult children and for parents who may have failed in their duties. Guide and bless them all, through Christ our Lord. Amen.

17. Prayer for Sick or Elderly Parents

God our Father, my parents are getting on in years. They are suffering some of the aches and pains and debilitation of advancing age. Sometimes they are so sick that all in our family get worried.

I love my parents. I would like to see them sound and well for as long as Your Providence will allow. Give them, merciful Father, relief in their increasing pains. May the doctors find out how best to be of help. May my parents receive the grace to offer to You through Christ, with Christ, and in Christ the sufferings that refuse to go away.

Give me, Lord God, that growing love of my parents which shows me how to be as near to them in their suffering as I possibly can. May my parents find in me a solace and a helpful loved one.

Mary Immaculate, help of Christians, intercede for my parents now and always. Amen.

18. Prayer When Leaving the House

I am about to leave our home in order to go (e.g., to work, to Church celebrations, for social events, on a journey, etc.). Lord, I am in Your hands. May every step of mine be a flower of love offered to You in the offertory procession that is my whole life.

You sent the Archangel Raphael to accompany the young Tobit on his journey.[37] He showed Tobit the way. He saved him from the destroying devil.[38] He indicated to him the bride You had prepared for him,[39] and he brought Tobit back to his parents to rejoice their hearts.[40]

Send, O Lord, my Guardian Angel to lead me, protect me, to show me Your ways, and to bring me home in peace and in joyful celebration of the success of my travel.

St. Raphael the Archangel, pray for us. My Guardian Angel, to whose loving care God commits me, guide, guard, protect, and bring me home in peace. Amen.

---

37 Cf. Tobit 5:4-16
38 Cf. Tobit 6:16-17, 8:3
39 Cf. Tobit 6:9-17
40 Cf. Tobit 11

19. Prayer Before Driving a Car

Lord God, You have enabled humanity to make vast progress in science and technology. The automobile is a clear example of such an invention. I am about to drive my car (to my place of work; for Holy Mass; for a social or other visit, etc.).

Guide my every movement so that I respect the traffic rules and observe all security measures for the good of other travelers, my family, and myself. I pray also that other drivers and pedestrians may do the same, so that none of them puts me in difficulty.

Lord God, it is tragic that many people worldwide die in car accidents or become injured. I pray for the most responsible use of the car and of the road by everyone involved so that injury and damage may be totally avoided or at least be drastically reduced.

Lord, in whom we live and move and have our being, give us greater security on our roads, through Christ our Lord. Amen.

20. Prayer Before Going on Vacation

Lord God, vacation time is a blessing for us. It enables us to get away from our daily work for a time, to find ourselves in different surroundings, to visit friends, and to be refreshed so that we can do our work better in the future.

Guide us, Lord, as we now set out on vacation. May our travel be smooth and trouble-free. May our contacts with other people be enriching and spiritually helpful. May our physical strength be refreshed so that on our return home we can better serve You and our neighbor.

We pray for those people who for one reason or the other are not able to go on vacation. May social conditions become such that they also can enjoy this opportunity.

God of all creation, to You be honor and praise now and for ever. Amen.

21. Prayer When Returning Home

You have enabled me, Lord, to be back home after my temporary absence because of (work; religious celebrations; social events; vacation; etc.). I thank You for enabling me to be back in my home where I belong, where I know I am loved and received, where I have the ordinary elements that enable me do my daily work, and especially where I have my family members whose society means so much for me in love.

Merciful God, bless our home. May I be the first to do everything in my power to contribute to its joy, peace, and harmonious functioning. May every member of our family share the same desires, concerns, and values.

Jesus, Mary, and Joseph, bless our home and every member in it, give us joy, peace, and a growing mutual love. Amen.

22. Prayer for Finding a Job

I know that it is Your will, O God, that we cooperate with You by our work in order to make this world a better place in which to live. Right now, I have not found adequate employment. I am looking for a job opportunity that will enable me to contribute my part to fulfill my duties to my family and society and to improve myself through my work.

Help me, Lord, to find work. May those who make the decisions in our country that affect work, employment, and economic development be led by the highest motives. May they craft policies that truly serve the general welfare, especially in order to safeguard the good of the poor and the unemployed and to guarantee families a decent wage and suitable housing.

Our Lady, Queen of the Family, pray for us. St. Joseph, head and protector of the Holy Family, protect us. Amen.

23. Thank God for a New Job

Lord God, You have recently blessed me with (a new job; assignment; promotion). It comes to me as a pleasant and welcome sign of Your providential care. Through this job, You encourage the little efforts You have enabled me to make through all these years. It also makes it a little easier for me to contribute to the good of society, and You give me more means to respond to my family, social, and other responsibilities.

Thank You, Lord, for this gift. Help and enable me to carry out my duties in this new office with efficiency, joy, and peace, and to do so to the satisfaction of those for whom or with whom I work. May I see this work as my participation in Your providential design of creation and preservation. It is also my expression of my solidarity with my brothers and sisters in the pilgrimage of life.

Help me Lord to work with a spirit of self-sacrifice. Bless the fruits of my work. At my time of retirement, may I be able to look back with joy, peace, and gratitude. Accept this offering, through Christ our Lord. Amen.

24. Prayer at the Start of the Day's Work

At the start of work on this new day, I turn to You, O God. In this work and through it, You are calling on me to contribute my part to the improvement of creation. You are asking me to show loving cooperation with my neighbor.

May I be honest and efficient in my work. May

those with whom and for whom I work be happy and grateful because of my contribution. May I myself grow through good work performance.

Lord Jesus, You were known as a carpenter's son in Nazareth. You worked with Your hands. You learned from St. Joseph. You helped to produce what was of help to the Holy Family and to the larger society.

May I have the proper attitude to work. May this attitude be shared by all in our work place and throughout our country. St. Joseph, pray for me and for all workers. Amen.

25. Prayer Before the Day's Study

Lord God, I am at the beginning of this new day of study. Your Providence has arranged that from childhood every human being needs much study, schooling, and training in order to come into possession of what generations before him have said, written, done, or made. Then the student has to learn to speak, write, do, and make.

Study is difficult. Help me, Lord. Guide me. Motivate me. Help me to be obedient towards my teachers. May I learn more and more to discipline myself and to get accustomed to learning. I also pray You to bless my parents, my teachers, the government, and all those who in some way contribute to the running of our educational institutions. May the fear of God, the beginning of wisdom, guide all involved in the work of education.[41]

This we ask of You, through Christ, Eternal Wisdom. Amen.

26. Prayer During Work

Lord God, as I find myself in the midst of my work this day, I raise my mind and heart to You. My work is my way of carrying out Your will and building up society. I want to offer all the best that the talents You have given me will allow me to give.

Bless my work, Lord. Accept it as my offertory gift to You this day. Unite my little efforts with the offering of Himself that the Lord Jesus made to You on the Cross. Through Christ, with Christ, and in Christ, may my little cross be found of some value for salvation for me, for my colleagues, and indeed for Church and society.

By the intercession of St. Joseph, the worker at Nazareth, may my work be found acceptable to You. Amen.

---

41 Cf. Prov 1:7; 9:10; Ps 111:10

27. Prayer When Work Becomes Difficult

God our Father, I find my work hard going. I want to do it all with love for You and for my neighbor. It is not all smooth for me. I find difficulties and challenges such as fatigue, occasional temptation to laziness, disenchantment because of routine and sometimes tension, a lack of understanding or cooperation in my relations with those with whom or for whom I work.

Come, merciful Lord, to my help. Enlighten me to see how I can make a fresh beginning each day. Help me overcome temptations to laziness and loss of interest by remembering the example Jesus gave us. Help me also cooperate more generously with the graces You give me. Help me to not reject them through sin or negligence.

May my relationships with my colleagues in the work place be blessed with greater harmony and joy. Lord, please forgive me my failings in this matter, and give me the joy and peace and the enthusiasm of one who knows he is offering You a sacrifice of praise through faithful carrying out of my daily duties.

For all these graces, I ask You, through Christ our Lord. Amen.

28. Prayer for Retention of a Job

Lord God, I am grateful for the opportunity You have given me to find a job. I am aware that there are many who are unemployed. I also know that some have lost their jobs for various reasons such as their employer's economic difficulties, introduction of more machines, poor performance by some workers, or some natural calamities.

Help me, Lord, to give and to continue to give of my best in my job. May those for whom and with whom I work be satisfied with my performance. Guard our country from those economic difficulties that cause unemployment. May globalization in the world be positively approached in each country so that the human person will remain at the center of economic planning, and that large companies do not eliminate small initiatives and family businesses.

God of all creation, I praise You through my work and offer You adoration and thanksgiving through Jesus Christ our Lord. Amen.

29. Thank God for Unexpected Success

God our Father, You have recently surprised me with a great success. I was not expecting it. As a loving Father, You look after us while we are awake and while we sleep. I bow in front of Your loving Providence. I thank You for Your fatherly care.

I have always been convinced that not even a leaf falls to the ground without Your providential design. Your detailed plan and care of me are very reassuring. You have promised me through the prophet Isaiah that even if a mother would forget her child, You will never forget me. You have my name written on Your heart. You know me by name.[42]

Accept, Lord, my profound gratitude. Keep me always trusting, loving, and humble. Anything good that I am or may have done is itself Your gift. Keep me always in that state of mind, through Christ our Lord. Amen.

---

42 Cf. Is 49:15-16

ॐ PRAYERS FOR DIFFICULTIES AND SICKNESS ॐ

30. Prayer on a Difficult Day

Lord my God, today has been a particularly difficult day for me.

> -I rose up in the morning without the best of health.
> -The verdict of the doctor is not very reassuring.
> -At work, I met with considerable misunderstanding, and some of it was my fault.
> -I might have reason to fear a loss of job or a denial of promotion.
> -My children at school are in trouble with teachers, gangs, or drugs.
> -There are increasing problems with money, and I do not know where to find the money to fulfill my duties to my family, the Church, and society.

I kneel before You, Lord, full of confidence and hope. You have assured us that all the hairs of our head are numbered and that Your Providence covers every detail of our lives. Come, Lord, to my help. Give me strength to change the things that I can change, patience to bear the situations I cannot change, and wisdom to know the difference. May my whole life be an act of faith and hope in You, through Christ our Lord. Amen.

31. Prayer for Strength and Patience in Trials and Difficulties

Lord God, I am faced with trials and difficulties of many kinds.

> -In the family, I see misunderstanding, tension, and sometimes the exchange of harsh words.
> -In the work place, I have to face fatigue, lack of gratitude on the part of some of my co-workers, and occasional unpleasant hints from my superiors.
> -In the larger community, I am in a difficult situation (e.g., with the tax office; with the police; etc).

I accept, Lord, my guilt in many of these situations. Repentant in heart, I kneel before You to ask for pardon and peace.

Not all the situations are entirely of my making. I pray for the improvement on the part of others that is required. I beg You for the strength and patience I need in order to bear these trials, and I offer them all as flowers of love to You, through Christ, with Christ, and in Christ. Amen.

32. Prayer When One Has Been Humiliated

Lord, I have recently been humiliated.

-I have offended my spouse with unkind words and been found guilty by mediators.

-At work, I have been reprimanded by my superiors, partly due to my own fault (but also because of the envy of co-workers who made false or exaggerated reports about me).

-Some of my business prospects have recently suffered a set-back, and I am embarrassed to admit to my family that I do not know how we will pay for some of our basic necessities.

You have rightly humiliated me, O Lord, but You can also raise me up. Please wipe away my tears. Give me happier days. Teach me how to accept my littleness. At the same time, save my family and others from too much suffering because of my inadequacies. Have mercy on me, O Lord, have mercy on me,[43] for You are rich in

---

43 Cf. Ps 57:1

mercy,[44] and Your kindness has no bounds.[45] Amen.

33. Prayer When Receiving Bad News

Lord God, I am greatly upset at the news that I have just received. I am shattered by news about:

> -the sudden death of my dear friend, colleague, or benefactor.
> -my loved one who has been involved in a serious car accident or diagnosed with a serious illness.
> -my being robbed or my being cheated in my office/house/business, etc.
> -my job being terminated.
> -another serious problem.

Lord my God, come to my aid.[46] I do not know what to do next. In my confusion, I fly to You for refuge. In You, the poor man places his trust. It is better to hope in the Lord than to trust in princes.[47] Lord, You are the answer for those who have no refuge. Save me in this predicament. As a child flies to his mother's arms, even so do I seek Your protection. Mary, help of the helpless, pray for me. Amen.

---

44 Cf. Eph 2:4
45 Ps 145:3
46 Cf. Ps 70[69]:1[2]
47 Cf. Ps 118:9

34. Seeing God's Providence in Trial and Difficulty

Lord our God, everything in my life these days has not gone as I would have wished. I am presently faced with difficulties, challenges, problems, and complicated situations. I come up against unexpected suffering, threats, dangers, and perplexing situations. In many of these situations, I do not find the solution. I do not know what is best to do. Many of my plans either do not work out or are unsuccessful.

Even so, I trust in You. I know that You love me. No detail of my life, present or future, is outside Your loving Providence. Jesus Your Son has invited all who want to be His disciples to take up their cross and follow Him. St. Paul has assured us that You will never send us a cross heavier than we can bear. Rather, You will always give us enough grace and strength to bear it.[48]

Help me today. I am faced with real trials and problems. Please, in Your goodness and mercy, give me light, strength, faith, and Your sustaining grace. I trust in Your love even in this dark night.[49] May a bright new day dawn soon to comfort Your servant. This I beg of You, through Christ our Lord. Amen.

---

48 Cf. 1 Cor 10:13
49 Cf. Ps 23

35. Prayer When Sickness Arrives

Merciful Lord, the doctor has told me that I am sick with (diabetes; cancer; high blood pressure; stomach ulcer; liver deficiency; or other disease). This is not good news.

You are the God of life and not of death. It is to You whom King Hezekiah had recourse in his sickness, and You added 15 years to his life span.[50] Your Son Jesus brought healing to many.

I kneel before You in prayer for physical well-being. If it is Your will, may I be restored to a clean bill of health. May the doctors identify exactly what is wrong and be able to find and apply an adequate remedy.

Not my will but Yours be done.[51] If it is Your will that I suffer for a longer time, may You be blessed. When the time has come for me to leave this world, may You be again blessed. Whichever is the case, please give me the grace, faith, and courage to accept Your providential design.

Mother Virgin Mary, pray for me now and always. Amen.

---

50 Cf. 2 Kings 20:1-6
51 Cf. Luke 22:42

36. Prayer When Terminal Sickness is Announced

Lord God, the doctors and nurses are doing their best. They are trying all the remedies that they know. They are saying that they may not be able to arrest the situation. Death may not be far away.

I am shattered by this news. I did not expect death to knock at my door so soon. I think at once of who will look after my family when I am gone. Additionally, I am afraid of Your judgment because of my sins.

Merciful God, I bow in front of Your inscrutable will. Please give me the grace to prepare for a good death. Send Your priest to bring me the comfort of the Sacraments. Give me peace and calm to conclude my earthly pilgrimage in Your love. Look after my dear ones left on earth. By the merits of Christ Your Son, our Redeemer, accept my sufferings and tears and have mercy on me.

Mary, Help of Christians, pray for me now and at the hour of my death. Amen.

∾ PRAYERS FOR VIRTUES ∾

37. Prayer for Love of Others

Lord Jesus Christ, You have taught us that what we do to others we do to You.[52] St. John has told us that he who says, "I love God," but does not love his neighbor is a liar.[53]

I find myself often selfish. I do not think enough of the good of my neighbor. I seem too preoccupied with myself and my own affairs. I do not show enough concern for people in need.

Lord Jesus, heal me of this weakness. You loved us so much that You gave Your life for us while we were yet sinners. Open my heart to my neighbor. Show me that my neighbor is my path to You. Give me charity, the distinguishing mark of Your followers.[54]

Holy Spirit, Lord of love, fill me with the fire of Divine Love, so that I may share that love with my neighbor. Amen.

---

52 Cf. Matt 7:12

53 Cf. 1 John 4:20

54 Cf. John 13:35; Cf. *Apostolicam Actuositatem*, no. 8, November 18, 1965; Cf. *Homily of Pope John Paul II*, October 13, 1989

38. Prayer for Humility

Lord, I extol myself too much. I think too highly of myself. I tend to look down on others. I even seem to forget that any good thing I may have done is itself Your gift. I expect too many marks of honor from people.

Merciful Lord, heal me of my pride. Teach me that whatever I am that is good, or whatever positive thing I may have done comes from You as a generous gift. Only my sins are totally attributable to me.[55] Lord, convince me that without You, not only I can do nothing, but I would not even exist or continue to exist. Pride should have no place in me if I recognize the nothingness of myself, and my total dependence on You.

Almighty God, You have put down the mighty from their throne and exalted the humble.[56] I come before You in dust and ashes. Please give me the grace of genuine humility.

Mary, model of the humble, please pray for me. Amen.

---

55 Cf. Rom 7:18
56 Cf. Luke 1:52

39. Prayer for Wisdom in Making a Decision

Lord God, I am faced with a difficult decision. It is not easy for me to know what will best lead to Your greater glory, to the good of my neighbor, and to my own good.

I beg for the light of Your Holy Spirit. Without His guiding light and strengthening grace, I would not know what is best to do nor have the courage to do it.

Disentangle for me, Holy Spirit, the different aspects of this situation that make it difficult for me to make the best decision. Show me Your way, Your will, Your providence.

Mary, Mother of Good Counsel, You were ever obedient to the hidden but powerful action of the Holy Spirit.[57] Obtain for me His light, His guidance in this perplexing situation. Amen.

40. Prayer for Courage to Confess the Faith in Public

Lord, I am faced with a situation where I have to take a stand for You in public. I am obliged to make a choice that should be my confession and profession of my Catholic Faith in front of other people. The consequences of such an action are not all clear to me

---

57 Cf. Luke 1:38

now. I might suffer ridicule, sneers, rejection, persecution, loss of promotion, unemployment, or even violence. My family could suffer as a result.

Give me courage, Lord. May Your strengthening grace show me what to say or do, and then grant me the courage to do it without fear. The consequences, I leave in Your fatherly hands because I know You care for me much more than I can provide for myself.

Lord God of power and might, to You be honor and glory, for ever and ever. Amen.

41. Prayer for a Healthy Attitude toward Material Things

Lord God, Creator of man and of all that exists, You have made us human beings in such a way that we need to have some minimum use of material things. Because of the consequences of original sin and my human weakness, I tend sometimes to be over-attached to the use of money, clothes, house equipment, cars, and other creatures.

Teach me, Lord, the right attitude towards material things. While I work to earn enough to fulfill my family and social responsibilities, save me from attachment to the goods of earth. May I learn to be content with little and to serve You with evangelical simplicity.

Lord Jesus, in Your life on earth You gave us a model of detachment from material things. Accept my humble prayer, for You are Lord and Savior of all. Amen.

42. Prayer in Moments of Sadness or Depression

Lord of all consolation, I am in one of those moments when I feel sad, downcast, and lacking in enthusiasm. I seem to be losing interest in many things. Nothing seems to work or to be able to brighten up my spirits.

O God, come to my aid. Jesus Your only-begotten Son is the visible manifestation of Your love for me and for all men and women. By the work of salvation, He brought us hope, joy, and peace. As followers of Christ, we should be people of hope and joy.[58]

Help me, Lord, to overcome my moments of feeling despondent and depressed, to remember the great things You have done for me and for all humanity. Give me the grace of being reassured of Your love, blessing, guidance, protection, and fatherly Providence.

Our Father, who art in heaven, hallowed be Thy name. Amen.

---

58 Cf. Rom 12:12, 15:13

43. Prayer for Readiness to Forgive Others

Merciful God, some people have offended me.

-Some have made false accusations against me and thereby damaged my reputation or my promotion prospects.

-Some have violated my rights over land, property, or company business.

-A member of my family has been badly treated by a "friend" of the family.

-I have been dragged into court over a matter of which I am innocent.

-Some people discriminate against me because of my religion, race, color, or place of origin.

It is difficult for me to forgive. But Your Son Jesus Christ has taught us to forgive our enemies.[59] On the Cross, He prayed for those who were crucifying and mocking Him.[60] St. Stephen prayed for those who were stoning him.[61] Give me, Lord, the grace to learn to forgive my offenders from my heart. I pray also that they may change their attitude towards me, so that we can all serve You in peace and joy.

To You, the merciful and forgiving Father, be honor and glory forever. Amen.

---

59 Cf. Matt 18:20-35; Luke 6:32-36
60 Cf. Luke 22:34
61 Cf. Acts 7:60

44. Prayer for Pardon

God our Father, in many ways have I offended You. I have not given You due thanks for all Your gifts. I have even boasted as if certain things I did were due to my own goodness. Worse still, in some cases I have chosen a creature instead of You. You know my sins and failings.

Moreover, I have also offended against my neighbor. I have not been sufficiently considerate of the rights of others. I have caused concern, pain, and sometimes even heartbreak to my neighbor. Not everybody finds me a pleasant member of the family or a likeable colleague in my place of work.

I come to You, Lord, repentant. I am deeply sorry for my offenses against You, infinite Goodness. I repent for my sins against my neighbor. May I, Lord, have the joy and peace of being pardoned by You and by my neighbor. Relieved of the weight on my conscience, may I be able to go in Your peace as a sinner forgiven.

To You, merciful Father, be honor and praise, now and forever. Amen.

❧ PRAYERS FOR SOLIDARITY WITH OTHERS ❧

45. Prayer for the Poor and Suffering

Lord God, many people are suffering from poverty in their housing, food, and clothing. They possess inadequate means to maintain a dignified life in their families. There are people who are not assured of even one good meal a day. Then there are the sick, the old, the lonely, the orphaned, and the imprisoned. All these people are waiting for brothers and sisters who will show them a sign of Christian solidarity in the pilgrimage of life.

I cannot be indifferent to their suffering. The Lord Jesus has taught us that what we do to such people, we do to Him.[62] Help me, Lord, to see what I can personally do to be of assistance to them, and give me the love to do it. Many of the problems are beyond me in what is required for their adequate solution. May individuals, associations, and governments that can do something about it rally to show solidarity to the poor and suffering, in the name of Your Son Jesus Christ. Amen.

---

62 Cf. Matt 25:40

46. Prayer for Generosity to the Needy

God of love, who loves us without measure, teach us how to love. Your Son Jesus Christ told us that the last judgment will be based on how we have shown love to people in need.[63] All through the centuries, many saints have distinguished themselves in the various initiatives they have undertaken to relieve the needs of the poor.

I find myself, Lord, not generous enough. I seem to be too preoccupied with my personal affairs. I do not dedicate enough attention to the homeless, the hungry, the poor, and the sick. I do not give enough from what I have received from Your hands.

Help me, Lord, to open my heart and my hands more towards the needy. Convince me that it is more blessed to give than to receive.[64] You are Providence, and I know that You never leave destitute those who give generously to their more needy brothers and sisters. God of love, may Your kingdom come. Amen.

47. Prayer for Conversion

Lord God, I am concerned about my friend or colleague. You know that he not set a high priority on

63 Cf. Matt 25:31-46
64 Cf. Acts 20:35

religious practice. For years, he has not gone to Confession and rarely comes to Holy Mass. He has complications in his family and human relations. My efforts to dialogue with him over religion have apparently not yielded much fruit.

Merciful God, I kneel before You in supplication for my friend. Touch him by Your powerful grace so that he will return to the authentic practice of his faith for which I knew him many years ago. Remove from his understanding and his will all obstacles to following Your ways. If I have myself at any time given him bad example, please forgive me, Lord. May my friend and I have the joy of sitting together again at the Eucharistic Sacrifice to adore and thank You. This I beg of You, through Christ our Lord. Amen.

48. Prayer of Thanksgiving for Those Who Serve Us Daily

Lord, there are many people who serve us daily. I think immediately of my parents and relatives and my colleagues in the work place. But there are also the police and security people who see that we are protected, the workers who supply us with water and electricity, the farmers who produce what we eat, the priests who look after our spiritual welfare, and the government and its agents who coordinate the good functioning of our earthly societies.

For all these people I want to thank You, Lord. Bless them for all they do for us. Reward them for their sustained efforts to answer to our needs. Give them the joy of knowing that the people they serve are appreciative of their role.

May I and all other citizens reciprocate their good deeds by lives of positive contribution to the common good. Bless all our societies with love, collaboration, harmony, and peace, through Christ our Lord. Amen.

49. Prayer for My Greater Cooperation with Others

Lord God, You have created us human beings with a social nature. Teach me that interdependence between people is a fact, that I need other people in order to become all that I can be, and that society cannot develop and be in harmony unless we human beings learn to work together.

I come to You, Lord, to beg for the grace of greater cooperation with others. May the members of my family find me a pleasant contributor to the good of the family. In the place where I work, may I be an asset for harmony and good relationships. Where there is tension, may I bring understanding. Where there is coldness, may I introduce warmth and openness of heart. Where there is a silent war, may I be an instrument of peace.

Lord, help me to examine my conscience and my performance, instead of blaming other people for unpleasant situations. You are the God of love, harmony, order, and peace. Guide me in all my associations with others. This I beg of You, through Christ our Lord. Amen.

50. Thank God for My Friends

Lord God, You have created us human beings with a social nature, and human interdependence is of Your design. Teach us that we humans cannot become all that we can be without other people, for it is in association with others that we can reach the height of our potential.

Human friendship is therefore in line with the nature that You have given us. May my association with other people always be based on mutual respect, Christian charity, and readiness to sacrifice myself for the good of others. May all my friendships be respectful of Your will. May I never treat a fellow human being as an object, but always as a person, as a subject. In full respect of Your providential design, may all my friendships promote Your greater glory and the growth of my friends and me in many senses of that word.

I pray, Lord, for those who have abused or damaged friendships. May they return to the design of Your loving providence, and may all my friendships be conducive to growth, joy, peace, holiness, and greater harmony in society.

This we ask of You, through Christ our Lord. Amen.

❧ PRAYERS FOR CHURCH AND SOCIETY ❧

51. Prayer for the Discernment of My Vocation

Lord God, in Your providential design You have foreseen and prepared a vocation for every man and woman. I pray for light to find out what You would have me do. Help me to see Your plans for me. With the help of my parents, my teachers, my spiritual director, and others who know me, may Your plan for me unfold clearly.

I need not only light to see Your will, but also courage and generosity to follow it and carry out its demands. I pray for constancy, discipline, and perseverance so that I may not fall short in my vocation through lack of my cooperation.

I pray also for all young people who are about to reach decisions on their vocation in the Church and in the world. May the light and strengthening of the Holy Spirit be with us all. Amen.

52. Prayer for Greater Love of the Church and of the Pope

Lord Jesus Christ, I believe You have given us the

Church so that the riches of Your work of salvation may reach all people at all times and in all places. Thank You, for in the Church You feed us with Your word and teaching, with the sacraments, with the witness of the Catholic community, and with the prayer life of the Church.

In the Church, I thank You because You have given us the Pope to be Your vicar on earth and the successor of St. Peter, to guarantee the unity of Your Church, and to lead us in following You. I believe that he is the head of the apostolic college, which he forms with the bishops in union with him.[65] Teach me always to love, respect, and obey the Pope. May all appreciate the contribution of his office to the good of the Church and society more and more.

Lord Jesus, keep Your Bride, the Church,[66] always without spot or wrinkle so that each day she will bear ever-greater witness to You and to the Gospel. Amen.

53. Prayer for Our Bishop

Lord Jesus Christ, I thank You for having provided for us in Your Church the ministry of bishops. I rejoice that in each diocese the bishop is Your vicar, the Chief

---

65 Cf. Is 22:20-25; Cf. Matt 16:18-20; Cf. Matt 18:18; Cf. John 21:15-17
66 Cf. 2 Cor 11:2

Priest to promote divine worship and lead his team of priests for evangelization. He ensures that the word of God is spread, preached, and shared. He promotes the organization of the Church in the diocese so that good witness can be given to You.

I pray for our diocesan bishop. Give him, Lord, the joy of seeing the work of evangelization make great progress. May he have the unflinching cooperation of his priests, deacons, and lay leaders. May the poor and the needy find in him a father who shows them the love of God, who never abandons them.

Lord Jesus, protect our bishop from all evil and from the hands of those who do not love the Church. Give him good health and the joy of looking back at a ministry faithfully carried out.

Lord Jesus, Eternal High Priest, bless our bishop. Amen.

54. Prayer for the Parish Priest

Lord Jesus, our parish is blessed with the services of a priest who celebrates for us the sacred rites, who preaches to us the word of God, and who gathers the people of God together under the authority of the bishop.

I pray for our parish priest. Give him, Lord Jesus,

deep faith, especially in the eucharistic mystery which he celebrates for us every day. May he be so filled with the Holy Scripture and with the teaching of our Catholic faith that we are well nourished whenever we listen to him. Our parish under the direction of our priest also wants to serve the poor and the needy. Give our parish priest the wisdom to see how best to lead us in this life of witness to You.

Protect our parish priest from all evil, especially from the snares of the devil. May he grow in holiness and find joy and peace in his ministry. May many young people be inspired by him to desire also to serve You in the priesthood or the consecrated life.

Lord Jesus, Eternal High Priest, bless our parish priest now and forever. Amen.

55. Prayer for Vocations to the Priesthood and to the Consecrated Life

Lord Jesus Christ, You never deny to Your Church vocations to the priesthood and to the various states of the consecrated life.

The Church needs more and more young men who are willing to answer Your call to the priestly life for the service of the Church and the world.

Men and women are also needed in large numbers for the consecrated state of vowed chastity, poverty, and obedience. Such consecrated people have given You excellent witness in the history of the Church. They have helped to raise our minds to the things of heaven. They have rendered a greatly appreciated service of assistance to the needy.

I pray, Lord, for an increase in vocations to these states of life. May families welcome new life and educate their children in a greater sense of dedication and service. May more young people be willing to make the sacrifice involved in these callings. I pray also for the perseverance of candidates in seminaries and religious houses of formation. Bless them all, Lord Jesus, for the spread of Your kingdom, for the Church and the world, and for their own spiritual good. Amen.

56. Prayer for Persecuted Christians

Lord God, I bring before You the situation of many followers of Christ who undergo persecution for the sake of their Catholic faith. They are not allowed a free practice of their faith. They suffer discrimination in their place of work and are denied the promotions due to them. In society, there are ways both subtle and blatant in which they are made to suffer because they are followers of Christ.

Some governments sponsor an ideology that does not favor or accept religion and the Church. Christians are driven into hiding. Sometimes they are sent to concentration or so-called "re-education" camps. Some have been killed.

I pray, Lord, for respect for the human person, especially in his exercise of religious freedom. May this right be acknowledged and respected in all countries. May persecuted Christians once more be able to enjoy their rights.

I pray also for all persecutors of Christians. May they be converted and come to the light of the gospel. May everyone freely accept Christ and live and share that faith. Amen.

57. Prayer for the Persecutors of Christians

Lord Jesus, You taught us to pray for those who persecute us. You gave us a powerful example from the Cross when You prayed to Your Eternal Father to forgive those who were crucifying and mocking You.

I pray for those who make things difficult for Your disciples, those who discriminate against Christians and those who engage in direct persecution of Your followers. May all such people be converted like Saul was on the road to Damascus. May they appreciate the value of Christian witness and how important it is to let people freely exercise their right to freedom of religion.

Lord Jesus, You gave Saul on the road to Damascus the grace of conversion. Give such grace to all persecutors of Christians today. May they regret their mistakes, make reparation for violated human rights, and themselves acknowledge You as Lord and Savior, to whom be honor and glory forever. Amen.

58. Prayer for the Conversion of Those Who Do Not Know Christ

Lord Jesus Christ, there are still millions of people who do not know You and who do not accept and love You as their one Lord and Savior. Christians are only one-third of humanity. There are millions of people who would have believed in Christ if someone had preached to them.

Accept, Lord, my prayers for the light of faith for everyone who does not know Christ and believe in Him. Jesus is the one and only Savior for all humanity. May all those who are not yet Christians become members of the Church and enjoy with us the fruits and benefits of salvation. May they fully share the abundance of the means to salvation with those of us in the Church.

I pray for missionaries that they may with courage and perseverance bring the gospel to the ends of the earth. Remove the obstacles on the path of the evangelizers. May everyone know the one true God and You, His only-begotten Son and our Savior. Amen.

59. Prayer Before Voting in Political Elections

Lord God, I believe that society comes from Your creating hands. Thank You for having made us in such a way that human society needs some organization in order to function well.

As I go to exercise my civic right to vote, help me, Lord, to see the seriousness of the act of electing our political representatives. May I see in a clear light the issues at stake and the type of candidate that should be elected.

Since it is important that everyone involved in the electoral process observe the rules in all honesty, help our country, Lord God, to make the entire process function well so that the best candidates may be elected and the common good be promoted as far as possible.

Lord God of justice and truth, bless our land with a mature and honest electoral process. Amen.

60. Prayer for Those Who Govern Us

Lord God, knowing that it is Your will that human society may have some people placed in authority to guarantee and promote the common good, I pray for the people placed in our government at all levels, from the local government to the national. May they have a clear vision of their duties and of the common good, together with the firm will to promote this good. Give us competent public officials who can effectively carry out programs that benefit the people. I pray for honesty in our public officials. May they all resist the temptation to enrich themselves in dishonest ways. May their hands be clean in the administration of public funds.

Lord our God, give to our rulers the joy of knowing that they have the support and collaboration of the people. May they and all the citizens grow in love, peace, development in its many dimensions, and harmony in society. Amen.

61. Prayer for Fellow Citizens

Lord God, the condition of society will more or less depend on the mentality and action of its citizens if the society is to develop and be marked by harmony, love, and peace. I pray for all the citizens of my country. May we all love the fatherland that gave us birth and nourishes us. May every citizen appreciate the importance of his or her contribution to the common good. May our attitude toward work be a positive one that can help build up our society. May just laws be appreciated and respected. May honesty be a characteristic of the citizens of this land.

Lord, I pray for the conversion of any citizens who may be dishonest, unjust, or in some way oppressive of others. May we all accept one another as brothers and sisters in the pilgrimage of life. May our life on earth be a beautiful preparation for eternal life in our heavenly home. Amen.

62. Prayer for Deceased Friends and Associates

Lord God, You have called some of our friends and associates out of this earthly life. They have gone beyond us, marked with the sign of faith.

Our faith in the Communion of Saints teaches us to pray for the souls of the faithful departed, so that they may be released from purgatory if they have not yet reached our longed-for home in heaven. I pray for my deceased fellow citizens and friends. By the merits of Christ Your Son, forgive them, Lord, any offenses that they through human frailty may have committed. Bring them soon into Your eternal light.

I also offer for the same intention the Masses in

which I take part, my other prayers, and the sacrifices that are part of my vocation and mission. May Our Blessed Mother intercede for them.

Eternal rest grant unto them, O Lord, and let perpetual light shine upon them, through Christ our Lord. Amen.

BASIC PRAYERS IN
ENGLISH AND LATIN

On June 28, 2005, in presenting the *Compendium of the Catechism of the Catholic Church*, His Holiness Benedict XVI urged all Catholics to memorize Christianity's most common prayers in Latin, the universal language of the Church.

In an effort to help fulfill the Holy Father's request, here are those basic prayers.

Sign of the Cross

In nomine Patris, et Filii, et Spirtu Sancti. Amen.

In the name of the Father, and the Son, and of the Holy Spirit. Amen.

Our Father/Pater Noster

Pater noster, qui es in caelis, sanctificetur nomen tuum. Adveniat regnum tuum. Fiat voluntas tua, sicut in caelo et in terra. Panem nostrum quotidianum da nobis hodie, et dimitte nobis debita nostra, sicut et nos dimittimus debitoribus nostris. Et ne nos inducas in tentationem: sed libera nos a malo. Amen.

Our Father, who art in heaven, hallowed be Thy name. Thy kingdom come, Thy will be done on earth as it is in heaven. Give us this day our daily bread, and forgive us our trespasses as we forgive those who trespass against us. And lead us not into temptation, but deliver us from evil. Amen.

Hail Mary/Ave Maria

Ave María, grátia plena, Dóminus tecum. Benedícta tu in muliéribus, et benedíctus fructus ventris tui, Jesus. Sancta María, Mater Dei, ora pro nobis peccatóribus, nunc et in hora mortis nostræ. Amen.

Hail Mary, full of grace, the Lord is with thee. Blessed art thou amongst women, and blessed is the fruit of thy womb, Jesus. Holy Mary, mother of God, pray for us sinners, now and at the hour of our death. Amen.

Glory Be/Gloria Patri (aka, Doxologia Minor)

Glória Patri, et Fílio, et Spirítui Sancto. Sicut erat in princípio, et nunc, et semper, et in saecula saeculórum. Amen.

Glory be to the Father, and to the Son, and to the Holy Spirit. As it was in the beginning, is now and ever shall be, world without end. Amen.

Come, Holy Spirit/Veni, Sancte Spiritus

Veni, Sancte Spiritus, reple tuorum corda fidelium, et tui amoris in eis accende.

V. Emitte Spiritum tuum et creabuntur.

R. Et renovabis faciem terrae.

Oremus

Deus, qui corda fidelium Sancti Spiritus illustratione docuisti. Da nobis in eodem Spiritu recta sapere, et de eius semper consolatione gaudere. Per Christum Dominum nostrum. Amen.

Come, Holy Spirit, fill the hearts of Thy faithful and kindle in them the fire of Thy love.

V. Send forth Your Spirit and they shall be created.

R. And You shall renew the face of the earth.

Let us pray:

O God, Who taught the hearts of the faithful by the light of the Holy Spirit, grant that, by the gift of the same Spirit, we may be always truly wise, and ever rejoice in His consolation. Through Christ our Lord. Amen.

The Shepherd's Voice Series

The Shepherd's Voice Series brings you the current teachings of bishops and cardinals on vital topics facing the Catholic Church today.

Catholics in the Public Square
Bishop Thomas J. Olmsted of Phoenix explains the public rights and duties of Catholics and what is appropriate for us to do within the secular realm. He also describes how we should seek to influence our nation and its political process in light of our Catholic faith.

A Will to Live
Archbishop José Gomez of San Antonio, Texas, renowned expert on death and dying issues, explains how to approach end-of-life issues and prepare for death in a way that is moral and consistent with our Catholic faith.

Draw Near to Me
Francis Cardinal Arinze explains the power of prayer, describes how to pray, and gives examples of prayers we can use for all of life's triumphs and challenges. This magnificent, user-friendly work will comfort and inspire anyone seeing an ever closer relationship with the Holy Trinity.

ORDER TOLL FREE:
Phone: 888-570-5182
Fax: 972-929-0330

MAIL TO:
Basilica Press
111 Ferguson Court, Ste 102
Irving, TX 75062

SHIP TO:
Name:_____
Address:_____
City:_____
State:_____Zip:_____
E-mail:_____
Phone:_____

PAYMENT METHOD:
Check ☐ Visa ☐ MasterCard ☐ Discover ☐
Make checks payable to: Catholic Word
Credit Card #:_____
Expiration Date_____/_____Sec. Code:_____

SHIPPING CHART
1-4 books -- $3.25   9+ books call for shipping costs
5-8 books -- $4.50   Call for bulk discounts

Qty.	Item	Cost	Total
	Catholics in the Public Square	$4.95	
	Católicos y Vida Pública	$4.95	
	A Will to Live	$5.95	
	Draw Near to Me	$5.95	
	(WI residents add 5.5% tax)		
	Shipping		
	Total		